KB244178

Woojin's Weather Show

Happy House

About Wise & Wide

- A systematic 6-level English reading program based on Lexile® measures
- Diverse and interesting topics chosen from the elementary curriculums of Korea and English speaking western countries
- Well-written books in various forms including fiction stories, descriptive texts, and classics retold
- The informative but original fiction stories grab your interest, leading to the easy and clear understanding of the educational content.
- Improve thinking skills with solid after-reading activities at all levels of the series.

Wise & Wide is a 6-level English reading program that consists of 60 books and each level is systematically divided by Lexile® measures. The Lexile® Framework for Reading is the most popular reading measuring system in American formal education curriculums and many English programs. Over 20 out of 50 states in the U.S. mark Lexile® measures directly on students' final report cards and over 300 well-known publishers adopt and use Lexile® measures.

Experience many kinds of readings written by professional writers from the U.S. and England. They used interesting topics that were carefully chosen after analyzing elementary curriculums from around the world including Korea, the U.S., England, and Australia among many others. Comprehensive after-reading activities including graphic organizers, speaking tasks, and After-reading Tests are ready for you.

Levels in the series and their corresponding Lexile® measures

Level	Lexile® measures	U.S. Grade
Level 1	Below 200L	Pre K - K
Level 2	190L - 400L	Lower Grade 1
Level 3	350L - 530L	Upper Grade 1
Level 4	420L - 650L	Grade 2
Level 5	520L - 940L	Grade 3 - 4
Level 6	830L - 1070L	Grade 5 - 6

* Smart Readers: Wise & Wide level 1 is applicable to the preschool level in the U.S.

* The source of the relationship between Lexile® measures and U.S. school grades: CCSS(Common Core State Standards) FOR ENGLISH LANGUAGE ARTS, APPENDIX A (2012, which is used by 45 states in the U.S.)

Topic List

	Level 1	Level 2	Level 3	Level 4	Level 5	Level 6
Book 1	Science>Biology: The hibernation of animals Story	Science>Biology: Living and nonliving things Story	Science>Biology> Animals & the Environment: Sea otters Story	Environment> Living with nature: The diver & the persimmon tree Story	Science>Biology> Animal: Amazing animals of the Amazon Story	Science>Biology: Germs, transmitted diseases Story
Book 2	Literature> World classics: Aesop's fables Story	Literature> Traditional fairy tale: Old tales about stones Story	Social Studies> Economy: To run a business to make and save money Story	Science>Biology> Plants: Photosynthesis Story	Science>Earth science: Earth's layers, earthquakes, volcanoes, and earth's atmosphere Report	Mathematics> Sequence: The golden ratio & the Fibonacci sequence Story
Book 3	Science>Physics: How shadows are formed Story	Literature> World classics: Peter Pan Story	Science>Scientific technology: Nanobots Story	Literature>Myths: World's creation stories Story	Literature> Legend: The story of King Arthur Story	Literature>Myths: Constellation myths Story
Book 4	Literature> Traditional literature: The Talmud Story	Science>Biology> Animal: Polar bears Story	Science>Biology> Animal: Mountain gorillas Story	Social Studies> Cultural anthropology: Amazing ancient cultures of the world Story	Science> Earth science: Clouds and weather Story	
Book 5	Social Studies> Ethics: Rules in daily life Story	Science>Biology: The five senses Report	Social Studies> Cultural anthropology: Astonishing festivals Report	Art>Music: Stories from two operas Story	Social Studies> World culture & history: The Renaissance Story	
Book 6	Social Studies> World geography & travel: Tourist attractions around the world Story	Science>Biology> Animal: Dinosaurs Story	Science> Astronomy: The solar system Story	Social Studies> People: Three great people who overcame hardships Story	Science>Scientific technology: The wonderful world of robots Report	
Book 7				Science & Social Studies> Technology & culture: Inventions from around the world Report	Art>Works of art: Famous paintings Report	
Book 8						
Book 9						
Book 10						

10 books in each level will be published.

How to Use This Book

•Before Reading

You can easily find the topic and what kind of story you are about to read.

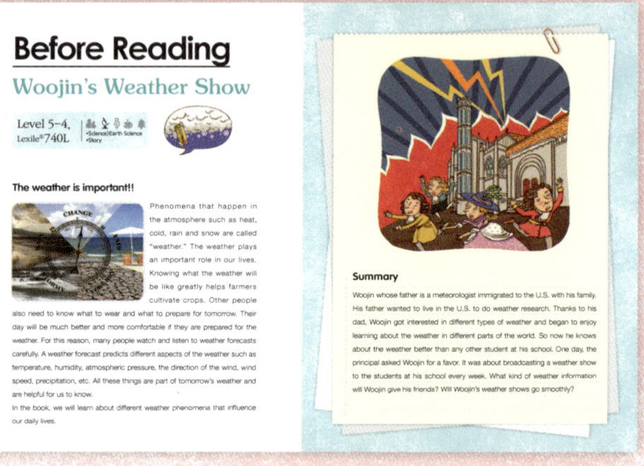

•The text

All the stories were written by professional writers from the U.S. and England, so you will read authentic and appropriate English sentences and expressions in every book in the series.

•Pop Quiz

Check out right away if you understand what you have just read by solving a pop quiz that checks your comprehension.

•Key Words

The key words and expressions on each page are listed for you to easily study them.

•Aha! Tips

Download free Korean explanations at *www.ihappyhouse.co.kr* for all of the sentences marked with "Aha!". These explain cultural, scientific, and economic knowledge or they deal with aspects of English such as grammatical structures or idiomatic expressions. There are lots of "Aha! Tips" to help you understand the text.

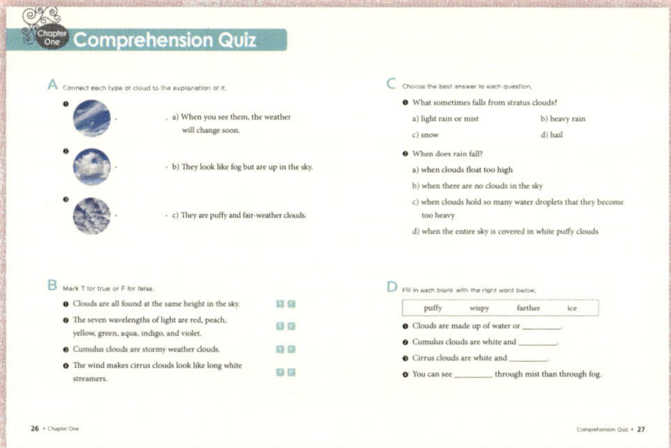

•Comprehension Quiz

After reading one chapter, solve various questions to find out if you fully understand the content.

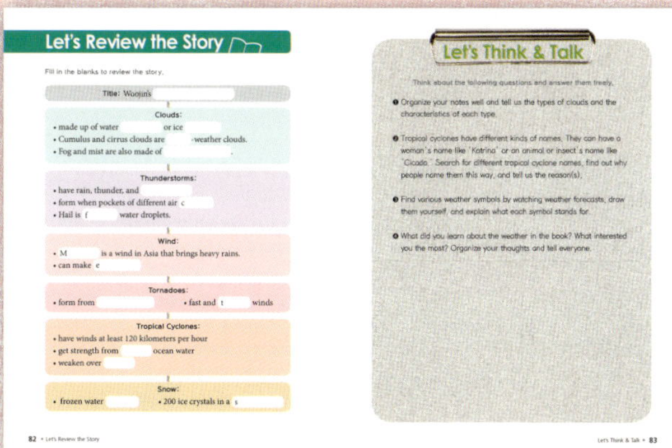

•Let's Review the Story / •Let's Think & Talk

Fill in the blanks in the organizer to summarize the whole story. Express your own thinking and feelings about the story by answering the questions. You can build up logic and reasoning skills for your essay examinations in the future.

Appendix

Audio CD
In the CD audio book form, the texts are read vividly by American professional voice actors.

After-reading Test
Solve an additionally provided After-reading Test for each book.

The Korean translation, Answer Keys, a Word Quiz, a Word List, and Aha! Tips for each book
You can download them for free at *www.ihappyhouse.co.kr*

Before Reading

Woojin's Weather Show

Level 5-4,
Lexile® 740L

- Science)Earth science
- Story

The weather is important!!

Phenomena that happen in the atmosphere such as heat, cold, rain and snow are called "weather." The weather plays an important role in our lives. Knowing what the weather will be like greatly helps farmers cultivate crops. Other people also need to know what to wear and what to prepare for tomorrow. Their day will be much better and more comfortable if they are prepared for the weather. For this reason, many people watch and listen to weather forecasts carefully. A weather forecast predicts different aspects of the weather such as temperature, humidity, atmospheric pressure, the direction of the wind, wind speed, precipitation, etc. All these things are part of tomorrow's weather and are helpful for us to know.

In the book, we will learn about different weather phenomena that influence our daily lives.

Summary

Woojin whose father is a meteorologist immigrated to the U.S. with his family. His father wanted to live in the U.S. to do weather research. Thanks to his dad, Woojin got interested in different types of weather and began to enjoy learning about the weather in different parts of the world. So now he knows about the weather better than any other student at his school. One day, the principal asked Woojin for a favor. It was about broadcasting a weather show to the students at his school every week. What kind of weather information will Woojin give his friends? Will Woojin's weather shows go smoothly?

Contents

Woojin's Weather Show

Woojin's Weather Show

Introduction

Woojin Loves Weather

Twelve-year-old Woojin loves weather. He loves gazing up at the sky and predicting what will happen next based on the shapes of the clouds.

Woojin was born in Korea. He and his parents immigrated to the United States when he was very young.

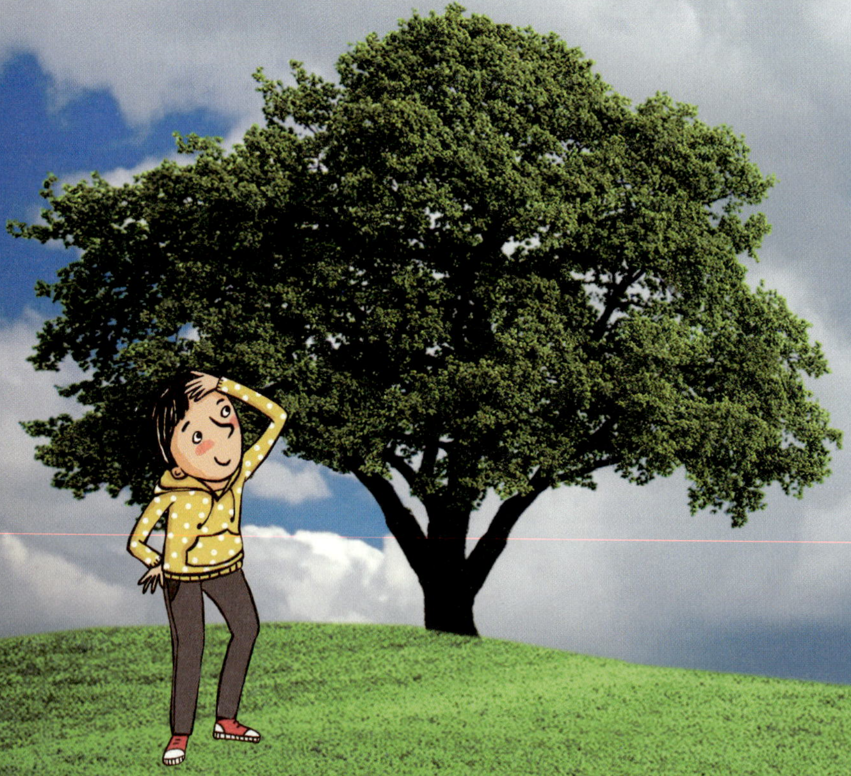

His father is a meteorologist, a scientist who studies weather. He wanted to live in the U.S. to study various extreme weather events, especially tornadoes. So they moved to California, and Woojin's father travels throughout the U.S. and studies weather patterns.

KEY WORDS

- gaze
- predict
- based on
- be born
- immigrate to
- meteorologist
- various
- extreme weather
- especially
- tornado
- move to
- travel throughout
- weather pattern

Woojin became interested in weather when his father showed him videos of tornadoes. No one in Woojin's family expected a video of tornadoes to turn into an obsession. Now, Woojin studies weather forecasts for different parts of the world and loves to learn facts about weather events that other kids don't know. 

Woojin's knowledge about weather attracted the attention of the principal of his elementary school. Mr. Sullivan asked him to do a weekly show at school to teach his schoolmates about weather.

KEY WORDS

- become interested in (become - became - become)
- expect
- turn into
- obsession
- weather forecast
- knowledge
- attract the attention of
- principal
- weekly
- schoolmate

Principal
Mr. Sullivan

Chapter One

Clouds

At this week's weather show, Woojin talks about clouds. Woojin knows clouds are made up of water droplets, ice crystals, or both, depending on the temperature of the air they float in. 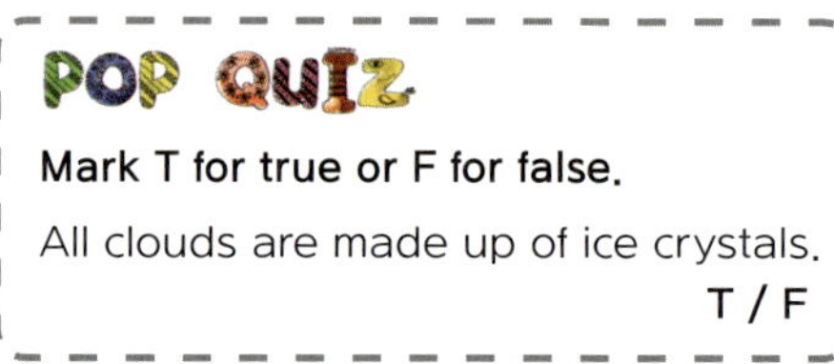

He also knows there are many different types of clouds. They often have complicated names. The clouds are found at different heights in the sky. Sometimes the names have to do with where in the sky the clouds are.

POP QUIZ

Mark T for true or F for false.

All clouds are made up of ice crystals.

T / F

KEY WORDS

- be made up of
- water droplet
- ice crystal
- depending on
- temperature
- float in
- complicated
- height
- sometimes
- have to do with (have-had-had)

▲ the variety of clouds

"Good morning, friends," Woojin begins his show at school.
He speaks to the entire school through the public address
system in the principal's office. "Do you know why clouds
are white?"

Sometimes a friend sits in the principal's office with him. Or
the principal answers his questions.

Today, Principal Sullivan joins Woojin in the office.

"Clouds are white because their water droplets scatter light from the seven wavelengths of colors. They are the same colors in the rainbow. Red, orange, yellow, green, blue, indigo, and violet wavelengths of light all exist in the color white," Woojin explains.

Woojin imagines his schoolmates might be confused. They might ask, "How can all of those colors make white?"

"They are colors of light, not colors of paint," he says. "If you mix all of those colors of paint, you will get mud. But light is different. It mixes to make white."

▲ the seven wavelengths of light

KEY WORDS

- entire
- public address system
- scatter
- wavelength

- indigo
- violet
- exist
- imagine

- be confused
- mud

▲ cumulus clouds

Woojin looks out the window. The sky is blue, and the clouds are puffy and white.

"Everyone, please look out the window. Do you see the white puffy clouds? Those are called cumulus clouds," he says. "They are fair-weather clouds."

KEY WORDS

- puffy
- be called
- cumulus cloud
- fair-weather
- pick up
- blow in (blow-blew-blown)
- cirrus cloud
- appear
- pause
- peek
- wispy
- streamer

As he watches, the wind picks up, and another kind of cloud blows in.

"Look again. Now we can see cirrus clouds," he says. "Like cumulus clouds, cirrus clouds appear in nice weather."

He pauses to give his schoolmates time to peek out the window.

"Cirrus clouds are white and wispy. The wind makes cirrus clouds look like long white streamers," he says.

▲ cirrus clouds

Woojin knows about lots of other clouds, but he doesn't
want to confuse his schoolmates.

"Cumulus clouds are made of water droplets and ice crystals.
Cirrus clouds are made of ice crystals because they float
higher in the sky where the air is colder," he says.

He peeks outside again and frowns.

"When you see cirrus clouds, the weather will change soon,"
he says. "So tomorrow we might see another kind of cloud."
He imagines his best friend, who often helps him with the
weather shows, looking confused again.

Woojin smiles. "These clouds are gray and usually cover the
sky. Sometimes light rain or mist falls from them. These gray
clouds are called stratus clouds." Aha!

Choose the right word for the blank.
→ Stratus clouds are ________.
ⓐ wispy
ⓑ gray

KEY WORDS

- higher
- colder
- frown
- light rain
- mist
- stratus cloud

▲ stratus clouds

Now Woojin wonders if he should stop his show here or talk about rain and mist. Aha!

Principal Sullivan speaks up for the first time. "Go on, Woojin. Tell us about rain."

"Rain falls when clouds hold so many water droplets that they become too heavy," Woojin says. "The droplets fall out of the clouds, and we feel and see rain."

"And rain falls from stratus clouds?" the principal asks. "Those kinds we see that cover the entire sky?"

"Yes," Woojin says.

> **POP QUIZ**
>
> **Mark T for true or F for false.**
>
> Rain falls when there are so many ice crystals in clouds and they become too cold.   T / F

KEY WORDS

- wonder
- if
- **speak up** (speak-spoke-spoken)

- for the first time
- **go on** (go-went-gone)

"Stratus clouds actually look like fog, but they are up in the sky," he continues.

"Then what is fog?" the principal asks.

"Like clouds, fog and mist are made of water droplets," Woojin explains. "They form closer to the ground when the air is cooler, like at night or in autumn."

"What is the difference between mist and fog?" his principal asks.

"Mist forms closer to the ground and is thinner. You can see farther through mist than through fog," Woojin says.

Since fair-weather clouds don't share the sky with stratus clouds, he and his schoolmates won't see any stratus clouds today. Maybe tomorrow. The weather changes all the time.

POP QUIZ

Mark T for true or F for false.

Mist forms closer to the ground and is thicker than fog.   T / F

KEY WORDS

- actually
- fog
- form
- cooler
- autumn
- thinner

- farther
- since
- share
- maybe
- all the time

▲ fog

▼ mist

A Match each type of cloud with the explanation of it.

❶ 

     a) When you see them, the weather will change soon.

❷ 

     b) They look like fog but are up in the sky.

❸ 

     c) They are puffy and fair-weather clouds.

B Mark T for true or F for false.

❶ Clouds are all found at the same height in the sky.    T F

❷ The seven wavelengths of light are red, peach, yellow, green, aqua, indigo, and violet.   T F

❸ Cumulus clouds are stormy weather clouds.   T F

❹ The wind makes cirrus clouds look like long white streamers.   T F

C

Choose the best answer to each question.

❶ What sometimes falls from stratus clouds?

a) light rain or mist   b) heavy rain

c) snow   d) hail

❷ When does rain fall?

a) when clouds float too high

b) when there are no clouds in the sky

c) when clouds hold so many water droplets that they become
too heavy

d) when the entire sky is covered in white puffy clouds

D

Fill in each blank with the right word below.

puffy	wispy	farther	ice

❶ Clouds are made up of water or ___________.

❷ Cumulus clouds are white and ___________.

❸ Cirrus clouds are white and ___________.

❹ You can see ___________ through mist than through fog.

Chapter Two

Thunderstorms

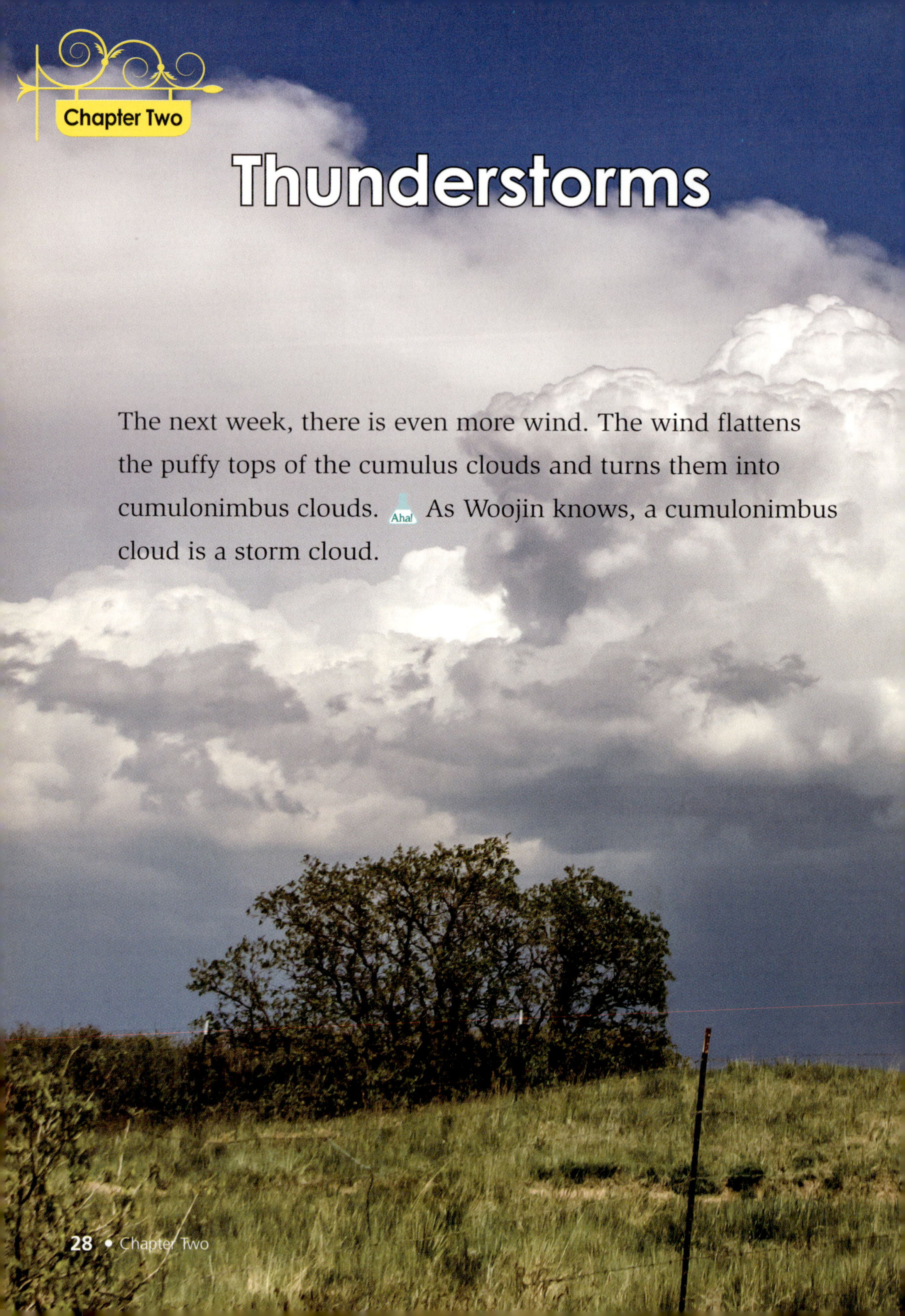

The next week, there is even more wind. The wind flattens the puffy tops of the cumulus clouds and turns them into cumulonimbus clouds. Aha! As Woojin knows, a cumulonimbus cloud is a storm cloud.

Today, Woojin's best friend, Kyle, joins him in the office. "Good afternoon, students," Woojin begins his broadcast. He speaks clearly into the public address system's microphone. "In the sky today you will see storm clouds called cumulonimbus clouds. They are big and gray, and they indicate that we will have a thunderstorm this afternoon."

KEY WORDS

- thunderstorm
- even
- flatten
- cumulonimbus cloud
- storm cloud
- broadcast
- microphone
- indicate

His best friend sighs. Kyle plays soccer after school, and a thunderstorm will cause his game to be canceled. *(Aha!)*

"I'm sorry, Kyle," Woojin says. "Those clouds tell the story. Don't count on playing soccer today."

"It isn't your fault, Woojin. You just tell us the weather. You don't create it," Kyle says with another sigh. "How does a thunderstorm form?"

"When a pocket of cold air meets a pocket of warm, humid air, we get a thunderstorm with heavy rain, thunder, and lightning," Woojin explains.

"Do thunderstorms always have thunder and lightning?" Kyle asks.

"Yes," Woojin says. "Thunder is essentially the sound made by lightning. You see lightning first because light travels faster than sound."

POP QUIZ

Mark T for true or F for false.

When pockets of warm, humid air meet, we get a thunderstorm. T / F

KEY WORDS

- sigh
- cause
- be canceled
- count on
- humid
- heavy rain
- thunder
- lightning
- essentially

▲ thunder and lightning, the two parts of a thunderstorm

"Is lightning just electricity in the sky?" Kyle asks.

"Yes, lightning is an electric flash. The electricity builds up in clouds and zaps toward the ground," Woojin explains.

"How is there electricity inside a cloud?" Kyle asks.

"Ice crystals in a cloud move around and bump into each other," Woojin answers. "The collisions create an electric spark."

"I've heard that lightning is very dangerous," Kyle says.

"That's true," Woojin agrees. "Lightning hurts more people each year than tropical storms and tornadoes. I'll tell you about those soon."

Kyle looks impressed.

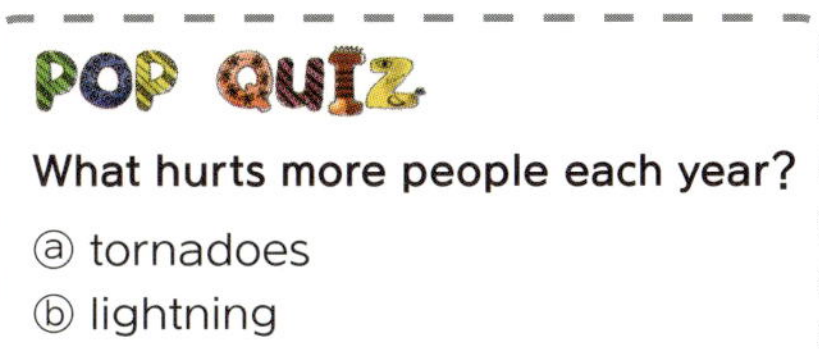

KEY WORDS

- electricity
- electric
- flash
- build up (build-built-built)
- zap
- move around
- bump into
- each other
- collision
- spark
- tropical storm
- impressed

"Did you know that a lightning strike is almost five times hotter than the surface of the sun?" Woojin asks.

"No way!" Kyle exclaims. "I don't ever want to get hit by lightning."

"Lightning may hit the Earth a hundred times each second," Woojin says. "That adds up to more than eight million lightning strikes a day."

"Wow!" Kyle says.

Woojin nods. "There are more than three billion lightning strikes a year."

"That's a lot of lightning," Kyle says.

KEY WORDS

- lightning strike
- **strike** (strike-struck-stricken/struck)
- times
- surface
- No way!
- exclaim
- get hit
- add up to
- million
- billion
- wild
- associated with
- vault
- gunpowder
- store
- start a fire
- destroy
- mouth drops open

"There are some wild stories associated with lightning," Woojin says. "Lightning struck a church tower in Italy in 1769 and went down into the vaults, where more than 90,000 kilograms of gunpowder were stored. It started a fire that destroyed one-sixth of the city and killed three thousand people." 

Kyle's mouth drops open.

"In 2005, lightning hit a house in northern England and set fire to a loft. The fire destroyed the owner's collection of *Star Wars* toys, which were valued at more than £20,000," Woojin continues.

"How terrible that he lost all of his *Star Wars* toys," Kyle says.

"Another thing that happens during a thunderstorm is hail," Woojin continues. "Water droplets rise higher and higher into the air to where the air is colder. The water drops freeze and turn into hail. When they become heavy, they fall from cumulonimbus clouds."

KEY WORDS

- **set fire to** (set-set-set)
- **loft**
- **collection**
- **value at**
- **£**

- **hail**
- **freeze** (freeze-froze-frozen)
- **mass**
- **a bit of**
- **average**

▲ hailstones

"Hail sounds like ice," Kyle says. "How is it different?"

"Hail is a large mass of ice crystals. Ice is a tiny bit of hail," Woojin explains. "Now I'm going to share some fun facts about hail. A town in Kenya gets the most hail. It averages 50 days of hail each year. Some years, it gets more than 100 days of hail."

"That is a lot of hail!" Kyle says.

"The largest hailstone in the United States was more than 20 centimeters across. It weighed almost one kilogram and fell in 2010," Woojin says.

"How do you get bigger hail?" Kyle asks.

"The biggest hail falls during the fastest winds," Woojin answers.

"Do all thunderstorms have hail?" Kyle asks. His curiosity is why he's the perfect friend to help Woojin with his weekly shows.

"Not all thunderstorms have hail," Woojin says. "To be considered a severe thunderstorm, however, there must be large hailstones, tornadoes, or great winds. Next week, I'll tell you about wind."

Choose the right words for the blank.

→ The largest hailstone in the United States weighed _________.

ⓐ almost one kilogram
ⓑ five kilograms

KEY WORDS

- largest
- hailstone
- across
- biggest
- fastest
- curiosity
- be considered
- severe

▲ Thunderstorms are accompanied by hail, tornadoes, strong wind, etc.

Chapter Two

Comprehension Quiz

A Circle all the things thunderstorms are composed of.

snow	rain
thunder	hail
fog mist	lightning

B Mark T for true or F for false.

❶ Cumulonimbus clouds indicate that we will have a thunderstorm soon. T F

❷ A lightning strike is almost five times hotter than the surface of the sun. T F

❸ Another thing that happens during a blizzard is hail. T F

❹ The largest hailstone in the United States was more than 200 centimeters across. T F

 Choose the best answer to each question.

❶ How many times does lightning strike the Earth in a year?

a) five

b) six hundred

c) one thousand

d) three billion

❷ A town in Kenya gets the most hail. How many days of hail does it average each year?

a) 10 days   b) 50 days

c) 250 days   d) 365 days

D Circle the right word(s) for each underlined part.

❶ Cumulonimbus clouds are (<u>big and gray</u> / <u>small and white</u>).

❷ Thunder is essentially the sound made by (<u>hail</u> / <u>lightning</u>).

❸ Lightning hurts more people each year than (<u>tropical storms</u> / <u>thunder</u>).

❹ The biggest hail is from (<u>the fastest winds</u> / <u>big clouds</u>).

Wind

Woojin thinks his schoolmates must know what wind is, but there may be a few younger kids who do not. 

"Wind is blowing air," he says at his weekly show. "Wind blows clouds across the sky."

"How?" Principal Sullivan asks.

"The motion is caused by the sun heating the Earth. Mountains, oceans, and other land formations make the surface of the Earth uneven, so the sun's warmth is absorbed unevenly. The atmosphere warms up differently depending on the land formations, too. Warm air is lighter than cold air, so it rises into the sky. The cool air replaces the warm air as it rises, so there is always moving air," Woojin explains.

KEY WORDS

- motion
- be caused by
- land formation
- uneven
- warmth
- absorb
- unevenly
- atmosphere
- warm up
- replace

Woojin realizes that his schoolmates might wonder why wind is important to the weather. "We could not have changes in weather without wind."

"That is true," Principal Sullivan agrees. "Wind moves the clouds and the air, and it brings temperature changes to different places. You've already told us how important air temperature can be."

"Right," Woojin says. "Last week I told you that thunderstorms form when pockets of air of different temperatures collide."

"I have a challenge for you, Woojin," Mr. Sullivan says. Woojin's stomach feels fluttery. He hopes that Principal Sullivan won't embarrass him.

Mr. Sullivan clacks the keys on his computer, and Woojin's nervousness grows.

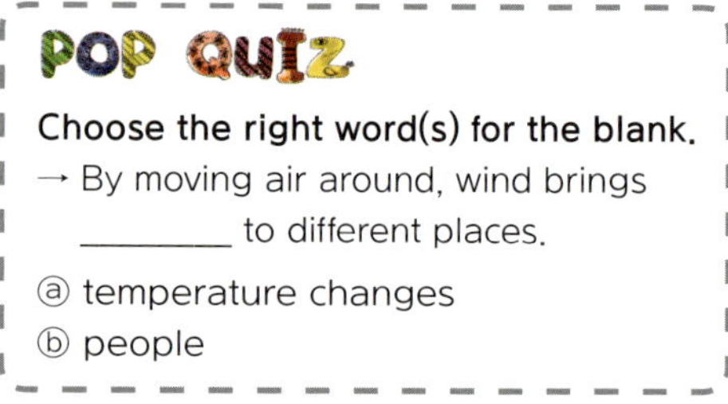

KEY WORDS

- realize
- **bring** (bring-brought-brought)
- collide
- challenge
- fluttery

- embarrass
- clack
- key
- nervousness
- **grow** (grow-grew-grown)

- windiest
- Antarctica
- reach
- per
- Good job.

"What is the windiest place on Earth?" Mr. Sullivan asks.

Woojin relaxes. He knows the answer. "Commonwealth Bay in Antarctica is the windiest place. The winds there reach 320 kilometers per hour."

The principal smiles. "Good job, Woojin."

"My family is from Asia," Woojin says. "In Asia, there is a seasonal wind called a monsoon. 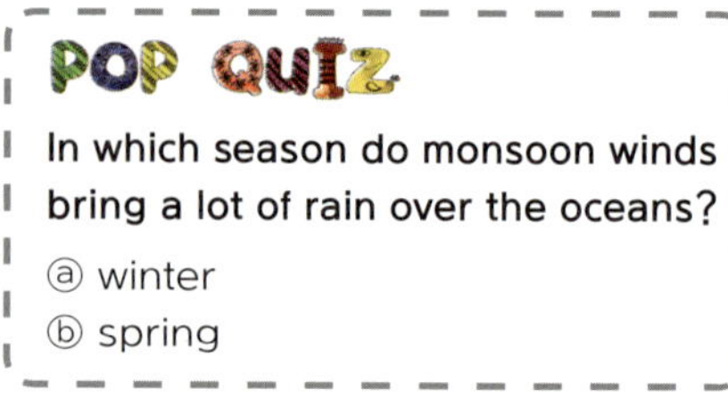 Monsoons often bring heavy rains."

Principal Sullivan nods his agreement.

"In summer, monsoon winds bring a lot of rain to the land. In winter, the winds bring the rain over the oceans," Woojin explains.

"Monsoons are serious," Mr. Sullivan says.

Woojin says, "A bad monsoon season brings torrential rain, tornadoes, floods, and landslides. Crops rot, and soil washes away. That leaves the land barren or unusable for months. Buildings collapse or wash away, which leaves thousands of people homeless. The worst monsoon ever killed 3.7 million people in eastern China when the Yangtze River flooded in 1931."

POP QUIZ

In which season do monsoon winds bring a lot of rain over the oceans?

ⓐ winter
ⓑ spring

KEY WORDS

- seasonal wind
- monsoon
- agreement
- serious
- torrential

- flood
- landslide
- crop
- rot
- wash away

- barren
- unusable
- collapse
- homeless
- worst

▲ a flood caused by a monsoon

"Nature is dangerous," the principal says. "Dangerous and impressive."

"Yes, weather causes many disasters," Woojin agrees. "There are also other winds like sea breezes, land breezes, and local winds with their own names."

Woojin continues, "A sea breeze is a local wind. It brings cool, refreshing air to summer afternoons. Land breezes happen at night. At night, the ground cools faster than the ocean."

"I have heard that wind is the most important new source of electricity in the world," Principal Sullivan says.

Woojin says, "Yes, it is. There is always wind, so there will always be wind power. Wind power leaves no dangerous waste products behind either."

KEY WORDS

- disaster
- sea breeze
- land breeze
- local wind
- refreshing
- source
- wind power
- waste product
- either
- do research
- capacity
- indeed

"I know," Mr. Sullivan says. "I'm very interested in the future of wind power, so I have done some research. The top three countries in the world for wind capacity are China, the United States, and Germany. What a world!"
Woojin agrees. Electricity made from the weather combines Woojin's favorite things. What a world indeed!

▲ wind turbine

A Mark T for true or F for false.

❶ Warm air is heavier than cold air. `T` `F`

❷ Thunderstorms form when pockets of air of different temperatures collide. `T` `F`

❸ The winds at Commonwealth Bay reach 3,000 kilometers per hour. `T` `F`

❹ Wind power leaves no dangerous waste products behind. `T` `F`

B Choose the correct word(s) for each blank.

❶ Monsoon winds bring a lot of rain to the land in __________.

   a) summer   b) fall

   c) winter   d) spring

❷ Land breezes happen __________.

   a) at sunrise   b) at noon

   c) at night   d) in winter

❸ A sea breeze brings cool, refreshing air to afternoons in __________.

   a) winter   b) spring

   c) summer   d) fall

C Solve the crossword puzzle.

Across

❸ where Commonwealth Bay is located

❹ a result of a bad monsoon season

❺ where the worst monsoon happened

Down

❶ a seasonal wind in Asia

❷ the most important new source of electricity

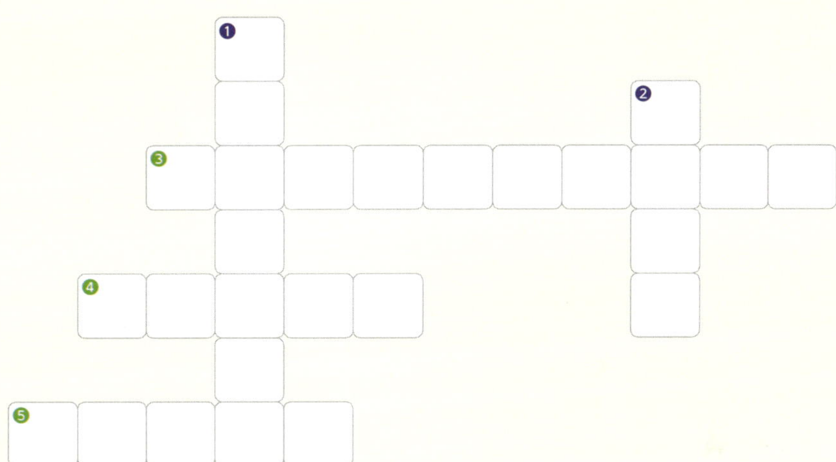

Tornadoes

The next week
comes, as does the
next episode of
Woojin's weather
show.
Low, gray stratus
clouds cover the
sky.

▲ stratus clouds

"Today I will talk
about tornadoes," Woojin says. 🧪 "Tornadoes are my
favorite weather topic and the reason I became interested in
studying extreme weather."

"Your father chases tornadoes for his job, doesn't he?" Kyle asks.

"Yes, he does," Woojin agrees. "He tapes big storms. They
are amazing. There are so many tornadoes in the United
States that my dad is always busy."

KEY WORDS

- episode
- chase
- tape
- amazing

"How many tornadoes are there in the U.S.?" Kyle asks.

"The U.S. gets around eight hundred a year," Woojin answers.

"Wow," says Kyle. "What about in Korea? Does Korea get tornadoes, too?"

"Yes, but Korea only gets damage from five tornadoes every three years or so," Woojin answers.

"Are there tornadoes everywhere in the world?" Kyle asks.

"Yes, there have been tornadoes on every continent except Antarctica. Antarctica doesn't get the warm, humid air that is needed for a thunderstorm. And without a thunderstorm, you can't have a tornado," Woojin explains.

"I bet you all would like to know what a tornado is and how it forms," Woojin says.

"Yes!" Kyle and Principal Sullivan say together.

Woojin laughs at their eagerness. "As I just mentioned, tornadoes form from thunderstorms. The most noticeable feature of tornadoes is their twisting winds."

"Isn't it normally a funnel cloud?" Kyle asks. He is full of questions as always.

"Some tornadoes have a funnel shape," Woojin says. "Some look chunky and smoky. Some have dust swirling near the ground. They come in different sizes and shapes. They can be narrow and ropy or look like cylinders or wedges."

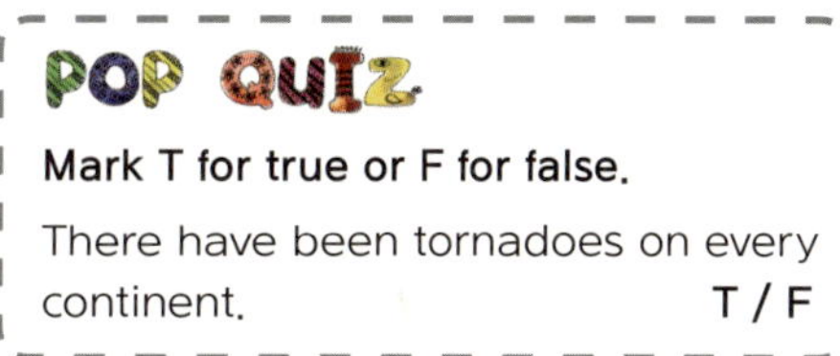

KEY WORDS

- damage
- or so
- continent
- except
- I bet
- would like to + *Verb*
- eagerness
- mention
- noticeable
- feature
- twisting wind
- normally
- funnel
- be full of
- as always
- chunky
- smoky
- dust
- swirling
- narrow
- ropy
- cylinder
- wedge

Woojin knows that a tornado's winds are really fast. "A tornado's winds are usually 160 kilometers per hour or less, but they can blow as fast as 500 kilometers per hour," Woojin says. 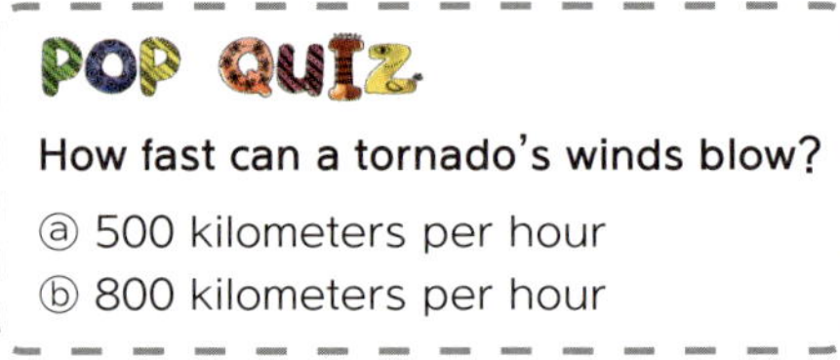

"How fast is 500 kilometers per hour?" Kyle asks.

Principal Sullivan answers, "The highest speed limit for cars and trucks on an American highway is about 137 kilometers per hour. Most trains in the United States travel around 240 kilometers per hour. A jumbo jet airplane, like a 747, flies around 800 kilometers per hour."

"Tornadoes are faster than cars and sometimes faster than trains," Kyle says.

"Right," Woojin says. "But not as fast as airplanes."

KEY WORDS

- speed limit
- highway
- jumbo jet airplane
- sure
- match
- debris
- in addition
- pluck off
- feather
- a bunch of
- toss
- far

"You told us about the largest hailstones in different places and some interesting facts about lightning. Do you have some facts like that about tornadoes?" Principal Sullivan asks.

"I sure do," Woojin replies. "The color of a tornado matches the ground and the debris it picks up."

"So it is usually brown?" Kyle asks.

Woojin says, "Yes. In addition, three-fourths of all tornadoes in the world happen in the United States."

"The winds of a tornado are the fastest winds on Earth," Woojin continues. "A tornado once plucked the feathers off a bunch of chickens. Another tornado picked up a train that weighed 83,000 kilograms and tossed it more than 24 meters."

"Wow, that is far," Kyle says.

"Tornadoes are also called twisters or cyclones," Woojin says.

He continues, "The deadliest tornado killed 695 people along a 352-kilometer path across the Midwestern United States in 1925."

"That's an impressive list of facts," Mr. Sullivan says.

Woojin smiles with pride.

"It is fascinating to learn about nature," Principal Sullivan says.  "Woojin, maybe one of your schoolmates will be inspired to study weather, too, because of your interest."

Woojin beams. He thinks everyone should understand weather. It's a part of understanding the world around us.

"Thank you, sir," he says. "Many weather events are also dangerous. You need to know about them so that you can protect yourself."

"That is a very good point, Woojin," Principal Sullivan says.

▲ a village destroyed by a tornado

KEY WORDS

- twister
- cyclone
- deadliest
- path
- Midwestern
- fascinating
- be inspired
- beam

Comprehension Quiz

A Circle all the words that describe tornadoes.

chunky

dust swirling near the ground

column of fire and smoke

funnel shape

smoky

square-shaped

B Mark T for true or F for false.

❶ Korea gets damage from about five tornadoes every three years or so. T F

❷ Without a thunderstorm, you can still have a tornado. T F

❸ Tornadoes come in different sizes and shapes. T F

❹ Three-fourths of all tornadoes in the world happen in Asia. T F

C Choose the best answer to each question.

❶ How many tornadoes does the U.S. get a year?

a) about twenty

b) about eighty

c) about eight hundred

d) about three thousand

❷ What is the most noticeable feature of tornadoes?

a) their color

b) their twisting winds

c) their height

d) the direction they move

D Circle the right word(s) for each underlined part.

❶ Antarctica doesn't get the (<u>high winds</u> / <u>warm, humid air</u>) needed for a thunderstorm.

❷ The color of a tornado matches the (<u>ground</u> / <u>mountains</u>) and the debris it picks up.

❸ The winds of a tornado are the fastest winds (<u>on Earth</u> / <u>in the U.S</u>).

Chapter Five

Tropical Cyclones

Woojin checks the sky before beginning his next show. The sky is mostly blue with streamers of white clouds.

Mr. Sullivan is out again, but Kyle is sitting and smiling next to Woojin.

"Today we can see cirrus clouds in the sky, so a change in the weather will happen in the next day," Woojin begins. "For now, we have nice weather. When there are cirrocumulus clouds instead, a certain kind of storm is on the way."

"That is a big word," Kyle says. "Cirrocumulus. It combines cirrus and cumulus. Do they look like a combination of those two kinds of clouds?"

KEY WORDS

- tropical cyclone
- for now
- cirrocumulus
- instead
- certain
- on the way
- big
- combination
- in rows
- puff

"Good question, Kyle. Cirrocumulus clouds cover the sky in long rows of white puffs," Woojin says. "So they are a combination of both wispy cirrus clouds and puffy cumulus clouds."

Now that he has explained the kind of cloud, it is time to talk
about the storm.

"Cirrocumulus clouds come before a tropical cyclone,"
Woojin says. "Tropical cyclones are storms that can be
965 kilometers across. They have winds that blow at least
120 kilometers per hour."

"That sounds like a very big storm," Kyle says.

"Yes, tropical cyclones are very big storms," Woojin agrees.
"These storms get strength from warm ocean water. They
eventually weaken over land."

"Is a tropical cyclone the same
as a cyclone?" Kyle asks.

"That's another good
question," Woojin says. "These
storms are called cyclones in
the Indian Ocean, the Bay of
Bengal, and Australia."

▲ the Bay of Bengal

KEY WORDS

- now that
- it is time to + *Verb*
- at least
- strength

- eventually
- weaken
- the Indian Ocean
- the Bay of Bengal

▲ the eye of the hurricane

"So they are called something else in other places?" Kyle asks.

"Exactly," Woojin answers. "They are called hurricanes in the Caribbean Sea, Atlantic Ocean, and eastern Pacific Ocean. They are called typhoons in the western Pacific Ocean, including Korea and some parts of Asia."

"I have heard of hurricanes, but what is the eye of the hurricane?" Kyle asks. Aha!

"The eye is the middle of the hurricane. It is the calmest part of any tropical cyclone," Woojin explains.

"I know you always have fascinating facts about the weather," Kyle says. "So can you tell us about the worst tropical cyclone in history?"

Woojin laughs. "Of course I can."

[Its birthplace: the origin of a tropical cyclone's name]

cyclone	in the Indian Ocean, the Bay of Bengal, and Australia
hurricane	in the Caribbean Sea, Atlantic Ocean, and eastern Pacific Ocean
typhoon	in the western Pacific Ocean, including Korea and some parts of Asia

KEY WORDS

- the Caribbean Sea
- the Atlantic Ocean
- the Pacific Ocean
- typhoon
- the middle of
- calmest

"The worst tropical cyclone in history was the Great Bhola Cyclone in Bangladesh in 1970," Woojin says.

"The cyclone caused a six-meter storm surge with winds that blew more than 225 kilometers per hour," Woojin continues.

"The surge hit the Ganges delta overnight and caused 300,000 to 500,000 deaths.  Seven of the nine deadliest weather events of the 20th century were tropical cyclones that hit Bangladesh."

"Wow," says Kyle.

Woojin nods. He finds weather fascinating.

▲ Ganges delta

Where did the worst tropical cyclone in history occur?

ⓐ in Bangladesh
ⓑ in USA

KEY WORDS

- storm surge
- Ganges delta
- overnight
- death

A Mark T for true or F for false.

❶ Tropical cyclones weaken over the ocean. T F

❷ The storm surge from the Great Bhola Cyclone caused 3,000 deaths. T F

❸ Bangladesh is often damaged by tropical cyclones. T F

B Choose the correct word for each blank.

❶ Tropical cyclones have winds at least __________ kilometers per hour.

a) 20 b) 60

c) 120 d) 400

❷ Tropical cyclones are called __________ in the Indian Ocean, the Bay of Bengal, and Australia.

a) typhoons b) cyclones

c) hurricanes d) tornadoes

❸ Tropical cyclones are called __________ in the western Pacific Ocean, including Korea and some parts of Asia.

a) cyclones b) hurricanes

c) tornadoes d) typhoons

C Solve the crossword puzzle.

Across ❷ one of the names for a tropical cyclone in Asia

❸ the name for a tropical cyclone in the Caribbean Sea

Down ❶ a kind of cloud that indicates tropical cyclones

❹ one of the names for a tropical cyclone in Australia

❺ the calm middle of a tropical cyclone

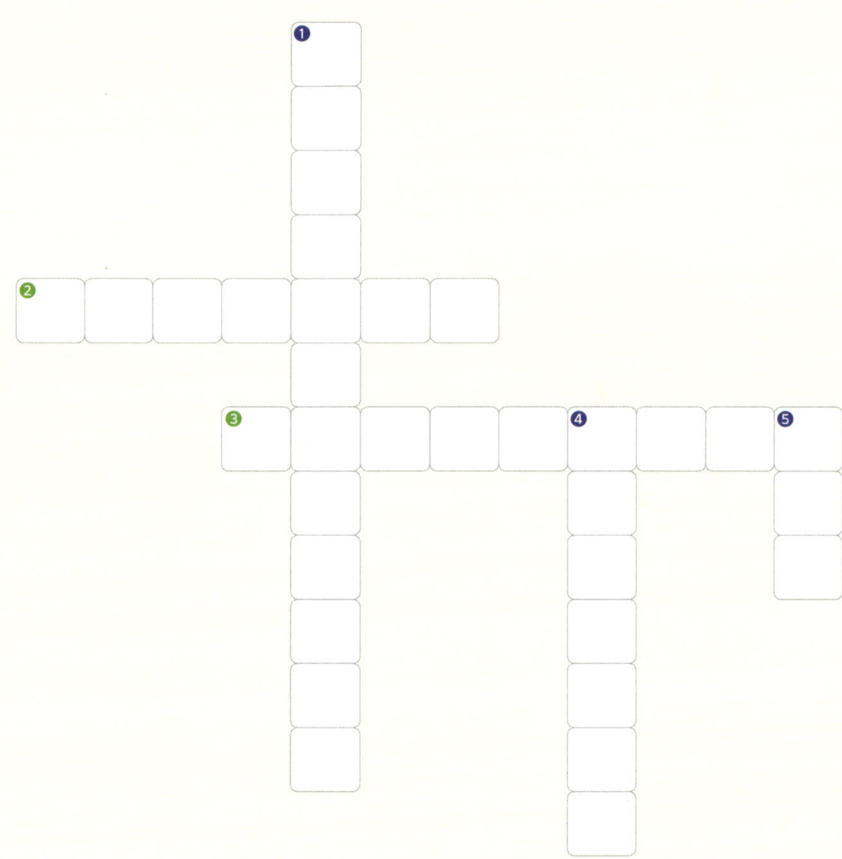

Snow

Woojin hasn't talked about winter weather yet, so he decides
to devote his next show to snow.

"Is snow just cold rain?" Kyle asks.

Leave it to Kyle to ask the funny questions.

"Snow falls from clouds just as rain does," Woojin answers.

"But it isn't frozen rain because snow is water vapor in the
atmosphere that turns to ice before it ever turns to rain."

"Huh?" Kyle asks.

Woojin laughs. "There is water vapor in the air all around us.
The more water vapor in the air, the more humidity we feel."

"When it feels humid out, is that because of the amount of
water vapor around us?" Kyle asks.

"Exactly," Woojin says.

KEY WORDS

- devote
- leave it to (leave-left-left)
- just as
- frozen
- water vapor
- all around
- humidity
- amount

"Does water vapor become rain?" Kyle asks.

"When water vapor fills clouds and they become too heavy, rain falls," Woojin answers. "But when the air is very cold, especially high up in the sky, water vapor freezes and falls as snow."

"I see," Kyle says. "How cold does it have to be for water vapor to turn to snow?"

"Zero degrees Celsius," Woojin says.

"Oh, right," Kyle says as he slaps his forehead.

"I bet you'd like to know why snow is white," Woojin says.

"Yes, please," Kyle says.

"Remember when we talked about why clouds are white?" Woojin asks.

Kyle says, "Yes."

▲ a snowflake under the microscope

"I told you that clouds reflect the seven wavelengths of light—all the colors of the rainbow—and together they all make white." Woojin raises his eyebrow at his friend in a questioning way.

"I remember," Kyle says.

"Well, the same thing happens with snow," Woojin says. "All of the wavelengths of light are reflected off a snowflake, so they leave the snow white."

POP QUIZ

Choose the right words for the blank.

→ When water vapor fills the clouds, it _________.

ⓐ turns clouds gray
ⓑ falls as rain

KEY WORDS

- zero degrees Celsius
- slap
- forehead
- reflect

- raise one's eyebrow
- questioning
- snowflake

"Then what is a snowflake?" Kyle asks. "Is it just a piece of snow?"

"Yes, you could say it's a piece of snow. A snowflake is made up of as many as two hundred ice crystals," Woojin says.

Kyle's eyebrows rise toward his hair.

"When the temperature inside a cloud is below freezing," Woojin continues, "ice crystals in the cloud surround a tiny piece of dirt carried into the sky by wind. When the glob of ice crystals is heavy enough, it falls as a snowflake."

"Snowflakes have dirt inside them?" Kyle asks.

"Yes," Woojin answers.

"That is much more interesting than a snowflake just being a bunch of ice crystals that fall from the sky," Kyle says.

KEY WORDS

- as many as
- below freezing
- surround
- glob
- snowstorm
- of all time
- You know it.
- bitterly cold
- take someone by surprise (take-took-taken)
- straight
- under the weight of
- for days

"Now I bet you want to know the worst snowstorms of all time," Woojin says.

"You know it," Kyle says.

"The seventh worst snowstorm ever was in Tibet in 2008," Woojin says. "Normally, Tibet is bitterly cold and doesn't get much snow, so this storm took everyone by surprise. The snow was an average of 1.5 meters deep and fell in some places for 36 hours straight. Many buildings collapsed under the weight of the snow. Seven people died, and roads were closed for days."

"That was really bad," Kyle says.

"The worst snowstorm in history was the Blizzard of 1967 in the Midwestern United States," Woojin explains. "The storm hit several large cities, including Chicago. More than 60 centimeters of snow fell, and winds blew more than 80 kilometers per hour."

"The snow must have blown around a lot," Kyle says.

"Right. And 76 people died in the storm," Woojin says.

"What a shame," Kyle says. "This show has been as fascinating as the rest, Woojin. Maybe I'll study weather one day, too."

Woojin decides it's time to ask his friend a question.

"So now that you know all of the amazing things that happen in the sky, isn't that stratus cloud up there much more interesting to you than it was a few weeks ago?" Woojin asks.

"Yes," Kyle says. "Even that flat gray cloud is more interesting now that I know it means storms are coming." Woojin smiles at his friend.

"Even though storms mean I might not get to play soccer today," Kyle says.

Woojin laughs. The weather is always changing. Today's storms will be gone tomorrow. There will always be another chance to play soccer.

KEY WORDS

- blizzard
- several
- around a lot
- What a shame!
- one day
- even though
- be gone

Comprehension Quiz

A Mark T for true or F for false.

1. There is never any water vapor in the air around us. `T` `F`

2. When a glob of ice crystals is light enough,
   it falls as a snowflake. `T` `F`

3. The seventh worst snowstorm ever was in Tibet in 2008. `T` `F`

B Choose the correct word(s) for each blank.

1. Snow is ___________ in the atmosphere that turns to ice before
   it ever turns to rain.

   a) clouds   b) hail

   c) ice   d) water vapor

2. The worst snowstorm in history was the ___________ of 1967.

   a) Blizzard   b) Cyclone

   c) Hurricane   d) Tornado

3. In the worst snowstorm in history, more than ___________ of snow
   fell, and winds blew more than 80 kilometers per hour.

   a) 6 centimeters   b) 60 centimeters

   c) 16 meter   d) 6 meters

C Solve the crossword puzzle.

Across
❷ the degree of Celsius at which water vapor freezes into snow
❸ the color of snow
❹ a bad snowstorm
❻ the site of the 7th worst snowstorm ever

Down
❶ hundreds of ice crystals surrounding a tiny piece of dirt
❺ the thing that a snowflake contains

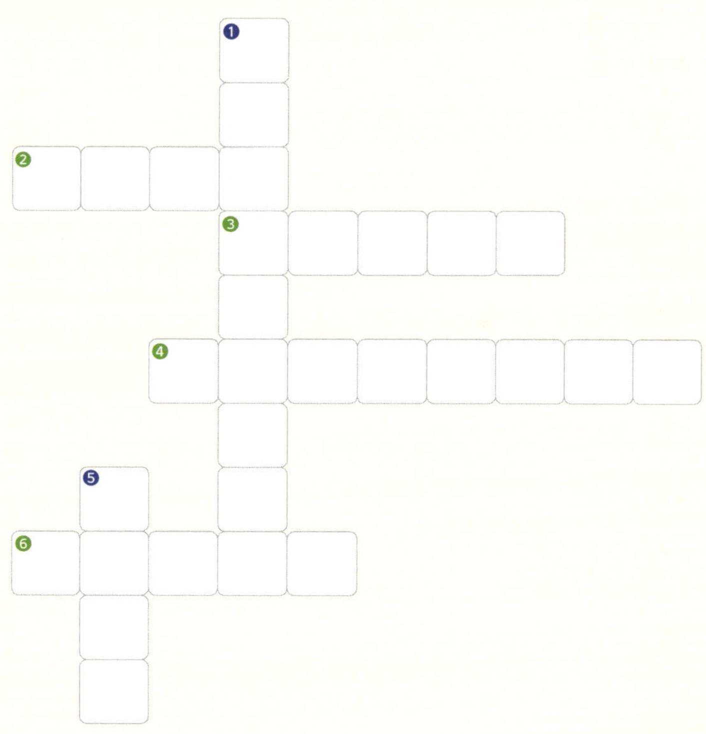

Let's Review the Story

Fill in the blanks to review the story.

Title: Woojin's ____________

Clouds:
- made up of water __________ or ice __________
- Cumulus and cirrus clouds are ______-weather clouds.
- Fog and mist are also made of __________.

Thunderstorms:
- have rain, thunder, and __________
- form when pockets of different air c__________
- Hail is f__________ water droplets.

Wind:
- M__________ is a wind in Asia that brings heavy rains.
- can make e__________

Tornadoes:
- form from __________
- fast and t__________ winds

Tropical Cyclones:
- have winds at least 120 kilometers per hour
- get strength from __________ ocean water
- weaken over __________

Snow:
- frozen water __________
- 200 ice crystals in a s__________

Let's Think & Talk

Think about the following questions and answer them freely.

❶ Organize your notes well and tell us the types of clouds and the characteristics of each type.

❷ Tropical cyclones have different kinds of names. They can have a woman's name like 'Katrina' or an animal or insect's name like 'Cicada.' Search for different tropical cyclone names, find out why people name them this way, and tell us the reason(s).

❸ Find various weather symbols by watching weather forecasts, draw them yourself, and explain what each symbol stands for.

❹ What did you learn about the weather in the book? What interested you the most? Organize your thoughts and tell everyone.

Let's Review the Story

Title: Woojin's **Weather Show**

Clouds:
- made up of water **droplets** or ice **crystals**
- Cumulus and cirrus clouds are **fair** -weather clouds.
- Fog and mist are also made of **water droplets** .

Thunderstorms:
- have rain, thunder, and **lightning**
- form when pockets of different air **collide**
- Hail is **frozen** water droplets.

Wind:
- **Monsoon** is a wind in Asia that brings heavy rains.
- can make **electricity**

Tornadoes:
- form from **thunderstorms**
- fast and **twisting** winds

Tropical Cyclones:
- have winds at least 120 kilometers per hour
- get strength from **warm** ocean water
- weaken over **land**

Snow:
- frozen water **vapor**
- 200 ice crystals in a **snowflake**

Smart Readers: **Wise** & **Wide**

After-reading Test

- Woojin's Weather Show
- Level 5
- 29 Questions

  (Vocabulary 7 / Reading Comprehension 16 /

  Sentence Structure & Grammar 6)

1. Which of the following is the wrong past tense form of the verb?
   ① set
   ② built
   ③ left
   ④ blown

2. Which of the following is the wrong comparative form of the adjective?
   ① colder
   ② thinner
   ③ interestinger
   ④ cooler

3. Which of the following is the wrong superlative form of the adjective?
   ① fastest
   ② bigest
   ③ calmest
   ④ deadliest

※ Choose the right word(s) for each blank. (4~5)

4.
> He is full ___________ questions as always.

   ① as
   ② of
   ③ to
   ④ off

5.

A snowflake is made ______________ as many as two hundred ice crystals.

① at   ② to
③ about   ④ up of

6. What is the common word for the two blanks?

• Don't count ______________ playing soccer today.
• He loves predicting what will happen next based ______________ the shapes of the clouds.

① on   ② to
③ for   ④ with

7. What are the proper words for the two blanks?

• That adds up __________ more than eight million lightning strikes a day.
• Sometimes the names have to do ______________ where in the sky the clouds are.

① for – on
② to – with
③ into – to
④ with – in

8. Which of these statements is true about clouds?
① Cumulus clouds are made of ice crystals only.
② Cirrus clouds are made of ice crystals.
③ Stratus clouds are white and usually cover the sky.
④ Sometimes light rain or mist falls from cumulonimbus clouds.

9. What are fog and mist made of?
    ① wind
    ② smoke
    ③ ice crystals
    ④ water droplets

10. What does the electric spark that causes lightning come from?
    ① ice crystals forming from freezing water
    ② water splashing in the cloud
    ③ ice crystals moving around and bumping into each other
    ④ hail colliding with mist

11. On which continent is the Commonwealth Bay located?
    ① Africa
    ② Antarctica
    ③ Australia
    ④ Europe

12. What speed do the winds in the windiest place on Earth reach?
    ① 100 kph
    ② 250 kph
    ③ 320 kph
    ④ 1,000 kph

    *kph: kilometers per hour

13. What do we call a seasonal wind in Asia?
   ① chinook
   ② cyclone
   ③ monsoon
   ④ hurricane

14. The deadliest tornado killed 695 people along a 352-kilometer path in 1925. Where did this occur?
   ① Antarctica
   ② Bangladesh
   ③ eastern Africa
   ④ the Midwestern United States

15. Which of these statements is true about tornadoes?
   ① Tornadoes are only narrow and ropy; they never look like cylinders or wedges.
   ② Tornadoes are faster than a car.
   ③ A tornado once pulled the beaks off a bunch of chickens.
   ④ A tornado's winds are really slow.

16. Where do three-fourths of all tornadoes in the world happen?
   ① Antarctica
   ② the U.S.
   ③ China
   ④ Bangladesh

17. What do tropical cyclones get strength from?
① cold water
② fast winds
③ the height of mountains
④ warm ocean water

18. Which of these statements is true about snow?
① All of the wavelengths of light are reflected off a snowflake. This leaves
the snow white.
② In the 2008 Tibet storm, no buildings collapsed due to the weight
of the snow.
③ When water vapor fills the clouds and they become too heavy, ice falls.
④ When the air is very dry, water vapor freezes and falls as snow.

19. Where did the worst snowstorm in history take place?
① Bangladesh
② Canada
③ the Midwestern United States
④ Tibet

※ Choose the correct word(s) for the blank of each sentence. (20~23)

20.
Mountains, oceans, and other land formations make the surface of the
Earth uneven, so the sun's warmth is ___________.

① cooled too quickly
② absorbed unevenly
③ disappeared
④ reflected evenly

21.

Cirrocumulus clouds come before a ____________.

① blizzard

② monsoon

③ tornado

④ tropical cyclone

22.

Tropical cyclones are called ____________ in the Caribbean Sea, Atlantic Ocean, and eastern Pacific Ocean.

① blizzards   ② hurricanes

③ tornadoes   ④ twisters

23.

Water vapor turns to snow at ____________ degrees Celsius.

① zero   ② ten

③ twenty   ④ thirty

※ Choose the wrong part of each sentence. (24~25)

24.

Now Woojin wonders if he should stops his show here.
         ①   ②   ③   ④

25.

Seven people died, and roads closed for days.
     ①   ②   ③   ④

26.

That is (interesting, much, than, more) a snowflake.

① much interesting than more
② more interesting much than
③ much more interesting than
④ more much interesting than

27.

It started a fire that destroyed (one, of, sixth, city, the).

① one the city of sixth
③ the city of sixth one

② one-sixth of the city
④ sixth one of the city

※ Choose the correct word for each blank. (28~29)

28.

Water droplets rise ____________ and ____________ into the air to where the air is colder.

① high, high
③ high, higher

② higher, high
④ higher, higher

29.

The ____________ water vapor in the air, the ____________ humidity we feel.

① much, more
③ much, much

② too, too
④ more, more

Brooke Rousseau

Brooke Rousseau is a writer, mother, and French teacher who strives to make the exotic familiar. Driven by a fascination with other cultures, Brooke has lived in Europe, Africa, and the United States, and visited parts of the Middle East and South America. She has earned degrees in French Literature and International Relations. Brooke writes nonfiction for older elementary children, short stories for very young children, and middle grade and young adult novels.

Woojin's Weather Show

Written by Brooke Rousseau
Illustrated by Minjin Lee

First Published in June 2015

Editorial Manager: Juyon Choi
Editors: Kyunghee Jang, Jiyeong Park
Designer: Eunhee Lee
Cover Designer: Eunhee Lee

Published and distributed by

Darakwon Bldg., 64-1 Jandari-ro, Mapo-gu, Seoul, Korea 121-894
Tel: 82-2-736-2031(ext. 250)   Fax: 82-2-732-2037
Homepage: www.ihappyhouse.co.kr
Publisher: Kyudo Chung

ISBN: 978-89-6653-195-0 18740 / 978-89-6653-156-1 18740(set)

[Components]
• 1 Audio CD (Recording Studio: Aram)
• Answer Keys & Korean Translation: Free download at www.ihappyhouse.co.kr